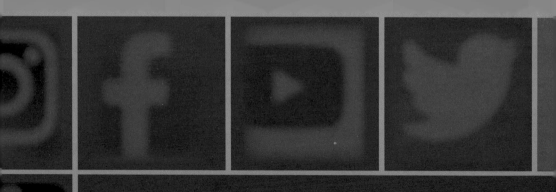

The Dark Side of
SOCIAL MEDIA

Bradley Steffens

ReferencePoint
Press

San Diego, CA

About the Author

Bradley Steffens is a novelist, poet, and award-winning author of more than sixty nonfiction books for children and young adults.

© 2022 ReferencePoint Press, Inc.
Printed in the United States

For more information, contact:
ReferencePoint Press, Inc.
PO Box 27779
San Diego, CA 92198
www.ReferencePointPress.com

LIBRARY OF CONGRESS CATALOGING-IN-PUBLICATION DATA

Names: Steffens, Bradley, 1955- author.
Title: The dark side of social media / by Bradley Steffens.
Description: San Diego, CA : ReferencePoint Press, Inc., 2021. | Includes
    bibliographical references and index.
Identifiers: LCCN 2021007484 (print) | LCCN 2021007485 (ebook) | ISBN
    9781678200787 (library binding) | ISBN 9781678200794 (ebook)
Subjects: LCSH: Social media--Psychological aspects--Juvenile literature. |
    Internet--Social aspects--Juvenile literature.
Classification: LCC HM742 .S833 2021 (print) | LCC HM742 (ebook) | DDC
    302.23/1--dc23
LC record available at https://lccn.loc.gov/2021007484
LC ebook record available at https://lccn.loc.gov/2021007485

Contents

Dangerous Words

On January 6, 2021, thirty-five-year-old Ashli Babbitt of San Diego, California, took part in a march on the US Capitol to protest the certification of the 2020 presidential election. Babbitt was one of more than one hundred thousand people to travel to Washington, DC, to demonstrate their support for President Donald Trump and the 147 Republican lawmakers who planned to vote against certifying the Electoral College tallies from the states.

Motivated Through Social Media

Like tens of millions of Trump supporters, Babbitt believed that election officials loyal to Joe Biden had tampered with the ballot counts in five states and illegally swung the election in Biden's favor. It was a belief advanced, cultivated, and repeated by the president himself. Neither Trump nor anyone else ever produced facts to support this supposed conspiracy. Furthermore, numerous state election officials—including several in the president's own party—dismissed these claims as false. Nevertheless, Trump made these unfounded allegations over and over, mainly through statements on his favorite social media platform, Twitter. Babbitt believed it was her patriotic duty to protest what she considered to be an illegitimate election. She hoped that an outpouring of support for the president would embolden Congress to stop the certification process and investigate the allegations of vote fraud.

The January 6 rally had been organized through social media, and most of the protesters were in touch with each other via Twitter, Facebook, and Parler. When Vice President Mike Pence, who was presiding over the Senate's certification session in the US Capitol, issued a statement that he was not going to overturn the election results, the message flashed through social media. Some Trump supporters were disappointed; others were enraged.

Fueled by Conspiracy Theories

Babbitt, who had served in the Iraq War and had once tweeted that Trump is one of history's "greatest warriors," was not finished fighting for her cause. "Nothing will stop us," she tweeted the day before the rally. "They can try and try and try but the storm is here and it is descending upon DC in less than 24 hours . . . dark to light!"[1] The words "dark to light" are a catchphrase for followers of QAnon, a far-right conspiracy theory spread mainly through social media. This conspiracy theory alleges, among other things, that a secret cabal had plotted against Trump all the time he was in office. True to her word, Babbitt joined with other Trump supporters and fought her way past police and into the Capitol. Once inside, Babbitt tried to climb through the broken glass of a barricaded door and into the chamber where the House of Representatives was meeting. A US Capitol Police officer shot her in the neck, and she died at the scene.

Five people died in the Capitol insurrection on January 6, including Babbitt and US Capitol Police officer Brian D. Sicknick. As the mob became violent, Pence gaveled the Senate session to a close and was evacuated from the building. House Speaker Nancy Pelosi was likewise hurried to a secure location. Other members of Congress were told to shelter in place and prepare to put on gas masks in case the police needed use tear gas to disperse the rioters. Eventually, the US Capitol Police escorted the senators and representatives to secure locations to wait out the siege. Hours later, after police and National Guard troops quelled

On January 6, 2021, a protest to contest the presidential election results at the US Capitol building turned deadly. The rally was organized via multiple social media outlets.

the disturbance, the lawmakers returned to their chambers and certified the election. By February 2021, 400 people had been identified as suspects in connection with the attack, and 135 had been arrested.

Silencing the President

Many people placed responsibility for the violence squarely on Trump and his tweets, including one issued during the riot that criticized Pence for failing to stop the certification process. Two days after the siege, the president posted two more tweets. One was a message of support to his followers. The other announced that he would not attend the inauguration of President-elect Biden. Those were the last two tweets Trump would be allowed to send. On January 8, 2021, Twitter deleted his account and announced that it would disable any accounts that served as a proxy for him. Explaining its decision, Twitter stated that the president had violated the company's rules:

> Due to the ongoing tensions in the United States, and an uptick in the global conversation in regards to the people

who violently stormed the Capitol on January 6, 2021, these two Tweets must be read in the context of broader events in the country and the ways in which the President's statements can be mobilized by different audiences, including to incite violence, as well as in the context of the pattern of behavior from this account in recent weeks. . . . We have determined that these Tweets are in violation of the Glorification of Violence Policy and the user @realDonaldTrump should be immediately permanently suspended from the service.[2]

Other social media outlets followed Twitter's lead. Facebook, Instagram, Snapchat, Twitch, and YouTube all suspended Trump's accounts. Believing that Parler, which had been used to organize the January 6 march, might give the president a forum to speak, Amazon removed the social network from its internet hosting service. Amazon stated that it took the action because Parler was not effectively moderating posts that advocated violence. Unable to find another hosting service, Parler went offline on January 11. Amazon, Apple, and Google all dropped the Parler app from their app stores, stating that it would only be reinstated if it did a better job of moderating its users.

> "These two Tweets must be read in the context of broader events in the country and the ways in which the President's statements can be mobilized by different audiences, including to incite violence."[2]
>
> —Twitter public statement

On January 13, 2021, the House of Representatives voted to impeach President Trump for "incitement of insurrection." During the then-former president's trial in February, House managers who prosecuted the case repeatedly cited Trump's tweets leading up to the siege of the Capitol as evidence of his role in the violence. Trump was not convicted, but the events of January 6 demonstrated the power of social media to influence opinion, galvanize supporters, and organize protests. And that power can be used for ill or for good.

Chapter One

Tearing at the Fabric of Society

In December 2020, as the first COVID-19 vaccines were becoming available in the United States, the Associated Press-NORC Center for Public Affairs Research asked US adults about their attitudes toward the vaccine. The researchers found that fewer than half of US adults—47 percent—planned to get the vaccine. Among those under age forty-five, the percentage was even lower. Only 37 percent planned to get the vaccine. The reluctance to get the vaccine presented a major public health problem. At least 70 percent of a population needs to be immune to a disease before it dies out. Reaching this level of immunity would be impossible without the cooperation of many of those who said they would not take the vaccine. The question is, why were so many people rejecting vaccination?

Scare Tactics

At least some of the concerns about the vaccine were related to false information that circulated on social media while the vaccines were being developed. For example, one meme claimed that the 50 million deaths that occurred worldwide during the Spanish flu pandemic in 1918 were not due to the illness but to vaccines that governments forced people to take. The meme added that the governments were repeating the same pattern with COVID-19 vaccines. The message is 100 percent false. There was no flu vaccine in 1918, so it could not have been given to people or killed anyone. The ominous ending of the meme was a scare tactic, designed to discourage people from taking the COVID-19 vaccine.

Another false vaccine meme featured two images of the rapper Drake, one above the other. The upper image showed Drake holding up his hand, as if saying no to the vaccine. Unlike the Spanish flu meme, the Drake meme did not exaggerate dangers of the vaccine. Instead, it understated dangers of COVID-19, claiming that the disease was thirty-three times less dangerous than experts believe it actually is. The meme states that the virus has a 99.97 percent recovery rate—suggesting that the disease is fatal to just three people out of ten thousand. The actual recovery rate is about 99 percent, meaning that one hundred out of ten thousand people contracting the disease die from it—a figure thirty-three times higher than claimed by the meme.

The lower half of the meme shows a smiling Drake accompanied by the words, "Alter my DNA from an experimental vaccine, with NO liability, from a corrupt industry."[3] Like many false memes, this one contains a grain of truth. The vaccine makers were shielded from lawsuits to help rapid development of the vaccine. And since the vaccine had never been deployed before, it could be considered experimental, although it had gone through rigorous testing and trials, just like other drugs. The most important claim—that the new vaccine alters a person's DNA—is based on the idea that the new vaccines use messenger RNA—also called mRNA. In at least two of the vaccines, mRNA enters the patient's immune cells and instructs them to make the spike proteins of the virus that causes COVID-19. The immune system recognizes these changed cells as a danger and destroys them. However, it retains a chemical memory of the spike structure, so the real virus can be recognized quickly and destroyed. After making the spike protein, the cell destroys

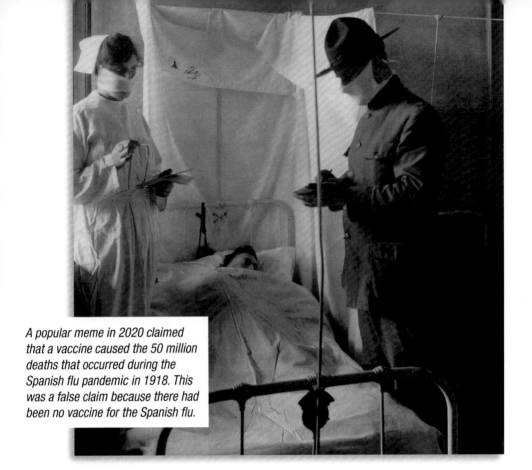

A popular meme in 2020 claimed that a vaccine caused the 50 million deaths that occurred during the Spanish flu pandemic in 1918. This was a false claim because there had been no vaccine for the Spanish flu.

the vaccine's mRNA and flushes it out of the system. During this process, the mRNA never enters the nucleus of the cell, where the DNA is stored, and it does not change the DNA in any way.

The Drake meme is not the only social media source suggesting that the vaccine changes a person's DNA, creating a type of hybrid human. This same false claim has also circulated on social media, thanks to the efforts of Carrie Madej, a Georgia osteopathic doctor. "The coronavirus COVID-19 vaccines are designed to make us into genetically modified organisms," Madej says in a self-produced video posted on BitChute. "We are entering into uncharted territory that can change what it means to be human."[4]

Alternate Sets of Facts

The COVID-19 misinformation does more than endanger plans for halting the spread of the virus. It adds to the widespread feeling that people do not know what to believe or whom to trust—not the government, not the medical establishment, and not drug companies. This confusion is tearing at the fabric of society. Rather than sharing a foundation of agreed-upon facts, Americans increasingly are adopting beliefs based on so-called alternate sets of facts. This is especially true in the realm of political debate. For example, both liberals and conservatives believe that global climate change is real, but far more liberals than conservatives believe that human activity is causing climate change. This disparity exists despite years of warnings by climate scientists and other researchers that human activity is primarily to blame for climate change. Because people do not agree on what is causing the problem, they cannot agree on the policies aimed at solving the problem.

The same is true in many other areas, from the effect of tax cuts on the economy to the impact of systemic racism on the nation's health and economic prosperity. People from all political groups acknowledge the existence of this fact gap. A 2020 survey by the Pew Research Center found that 80 percent of all US adults—regardless of their political affiliations—believe that people today not only disagree about political policies, they also disagree about the facts underlying those policies. This breakdown of a consensus about what is true and what is false is driving people apart.

A Lack of Editorial Oversight

Social media is playing a role in widening the fact gap because it makes it easy for partisans on both sides to spread misinformation. Traditional media outlets such as newspapers, magazines, and news websites have editors and fact-checkers who make sure information is accurate before it is published. Social media, by contrast, allows individuals to post anything they want, with only a few exceptions. The lack of editorial control enables social media users to spread false information. As a result, many ideas that might never have gained an audience are widely seen and oftentimes accepted as true. "The major new challenge in reporting news is the new shape of truth," says Kevin Kelly, cofounder of *Wired* magazine. "Truth is no longer dictated by authorities, but is networked by peers. For every fact there is a counterfact and all these counterfacts and facts look identical online, which is confusing to most people."[5]

Another factor driving the breakdown in agreed-upon facts is the popularity of social media as a source of news and information. If only a small number of people got their news from social media, the scope of the disinformation problem would be limited. But social media is the primary source of news among adults age eighteen to twenty-nine, according to a 2020 Pew Research Center study. Because of this large following among younger adults, social media has surpassed print media as a primary source of news for many US adults.

The Effects of Disinformation

The disinformation absorbed by social media users affects their knowledge of real events in a way that can be measured. According to a July 2020 Pew Research Center survey, those who depend on social media for political news knew less about political events than did people who got their news from other sources. The survey included nine questions about basic political issues, including which political party supports particular policies. People who correctly answered eight or nine questions were rated with high knowledge. About 45 percent of those who get their news mainly from news websites displayed high levels of knowledge, while only 17 percent of those who get their news from social media achieved the high rating. Such low levels of political knowledge pose a danger to the democratic process itself. "On page one of any political science textbook it will say that democracy relies on people being informed about the issues so they can

What Happens When People Rely on Social Media for News?

People who get most of their political news from social media know less about major current events and politics than those who get news from other sources. This is the finding of a Pew Research Center survey that was published in July 2020. As part of the survey, participants were asked nine questions that focused on basic political knowledge. Topics included the federal budget deficit and political party positions on certain policies. Those who get their news from news websites and apps or from radio or print news were shown to have much higher political knowledge than those who primarily get their news from social media.

Percent of US adults who have _____, according to an index of nine knowledge questions

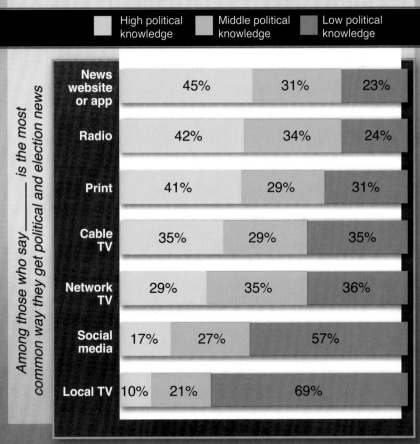

Legend:
- High political knowledge
- Middle political knowledge
- Low political knowledge

Among those who say _____ is the most common way they get political and election news

Source	High	Middle	Low
News website or app	45%	31%	23%
Radio	42%	34%	24%
Print	41%	29%	31%
Cable TV	35%	29%	35%
Network TV	29%	35%	36%
Social media	17%	27%	57%
Local TV	10%	21%	69%

Note: Knowledge index created from nine political knowledge questions. High political knowledge includes those who answered eight or nine questions correctly, middle knowledge includes those who answered six or seven questions correctly, and low knowledge includes those who answered five or fewer questions correctly.

Source: Amy Mitchell et al., "Americans Who Mainly Get Their News on Social Media Are Less Engaged, Less Knowledgeable," Pew Research Center, July 30, 2020. www.journalism.org.

have a debate and make a decision," says Stephan Lewandowsky, a cognitive scientist at the University of Bristol in the United Kingdom, who studies the effects of misinformation. "Having a large number of people in a society who are misinformed and have their own set of facts is absolutely devastating and extremely difficult to cope with."[6]

When it comes to conspiracy theories, people who get their news from social media are the most knowledgeable, according to the Pew Research Center. For example, 81 percent of those who get their news from social media had heard at least a little about the conspiracy theory that powerful people intentionally planned the COVID-19 pandemic, and 26 percent had heard a lot about it. This was a significantly higher percentage than those who get their news from television, radio, print, or online news media.

Social Media Companies Take Action

Social media companies have begun cracking down on the spread of false information on their platforms. Twitter, Facebook, YouTube, and Instagram have all enacted policies to remove or flag information they deem to be false. These actions are performed in part by human beings who fact-check content and in part by computers that use artificial intelligence (AI) software to identify which posts contain the false information. For example, in December 2020 a meme attributed to conservative activist Laurice Mitchell listed thirty-six expenditures included in the second COVID-19 relief package passed by Congress. The headline on the meme said, "Let's read line 17 out together." The seventeenth line stated, "$25,000,000 for additional salary for House of Representatives." Facebook covered the meme with a gray

14

screen that stated, "False Information. The same information was checked in another post by independent fact-checkers." The gray screen included two icons, one to remove the screen and view the meme and another to see why the post was flagged. Facebook placed a box labeled "Related Articles" beneath the post. This box contained a link to a story in *USA Today* entitled "Fact check: Coronavirus relief package does not include congressional pay raise,"[7] so viewers of the post could read why the information in the post was false.

Similarly, Twitter flags posts containing information it considers false or misleading with a light blue exclamation point and a statement, also in blue, explaining what is wrong with the tweet. For example, on December 28, 2020, Trump tweeted, "Breaking News: In Pennsylvania there were 205,000 more votes than there were voters. This alone flips the state to President Trump."[8] Twitter flagged the tweet and stated, "Election officials have certified Joe Biden as

The Bill Gates Microchip Rumor

One of the most widely circulated rumors about the COVID-19 vaccines involves Microsoft founder Bill Gates. A meme shows an image of Gates and the words "It's simple, we manipulate your DNA with a vaccine, implant you with a [computer] chip, make society cashless and put all money on the chip. Then you will do exactly as you're told or we turn off your chip and you starve until you decide you're ready to be obedient again."

According to a YouGov poll of 1,640 US adults in May 2020, 28 percent of those surveyed believed that Gates wanted to use vaccines to implant microchips in people. The meme grew out of a statement Gates made on the social media site Reddit. Discussing how to know whether people have had the COVID-19 vaccine, Gates revealed that his foundation was working on creating digital certificates that would show who has received a vaccine. Such certificates would be made up of chemicals injected under the skin along with the vaccine. The chemicals would store a person's vaccine records. The digital signature would not be a microchip, but the rumor started anyway and spread to millions through social media.

Quoted in Flora Carmichael and Jack Goodman, "Vaccine Rumours Debunked: Microchips, 'Altered DNA' and More," BBC, December 2, 2020. www.bbc.com.

the winner of the U.S. Presidential election."[9] Such comments on the president's tweets were a common occurrence in 2020. On November 8, 2020, Twitter flagged six of the president's tweets, four with the words "This claim about election fraud is disputed" and two with the words "Learn how voting by mail is safe and secure."[10]

Flagging disinformation is becoming commonplace in social media. In testimony before Congress on November 17, 2020, Twitter chief executive officer (CEO) Jack Dorsey stated that during the run-up to the 2020 presidential election and shortly afterward, Twitter flagged roughly three hundred thousand tweets for content that was disputed and potentially misleading. Facebook CEO Mark Zuckerberg testified that his company placed warnings on more than 150 million posts that independent fact-checkers found to be misleading. Two days after the election, Facebook banned a 350,000-member group called Stop the Steal that was attempting to organize protests against the prolonged vote count in key battleground states.

Free Speech Concerns

The flagging of controversial social media expression and the suppression of unpopular groups runs contrary to the tradition of free speech in the United States. This tradition holds that all speech should be allowed to compete in a free marketplace of ideas and that listeners or readers will decide what is true and what is false. Embracing this theory, the US Supreme Court has said that false speech is protected by the First Amendment of the Constitution. "Erroneous statement is inevitable in free debate," wrote Supreme Court justice William Brennan in the 1964 case *New York Times Co. v. Sullivan*, "and . . . it must be protected if the freedoms of expression are to have the 'breathing space' that they 'need . . . to sur-

"Erroneous statement is inevitable in free debate, and . . . it must be protected if the freedoms of expression are to have the 'breathing space' that they 'need . . . to survive.'"[11]

—William Brennan, Supreme Court justice

Twitter flags posts containing information it considers false or misleading with a blue exclamation point. In late December 2020, Twitter flagged six of President Trump's tweets about election fraud.

vive.'"[11] In his opinion, Brennan referred to the high court's earlier finding in the 1940 case *Cantwell v. Connecticut*:

> In the realm of religious faith, and in that of political belief, sharp differences arise. In both fields the tenets of one man may seem the rankest error to his neighbor. To persuade others to his own point of view, the pleader, as we know, at times, resorts to exaggeration, . . . and even to false statement. But the people of this nation have ordained in the light of history, that, in spite of the probability of excesses and abuses, these liberties are, in the long view, essential to enlightened opinion and right conduct on the part of the citizens of a democracy.[12]

Generally speaking, the First Amendment applies to governmental restrictions on free speech, not to limits placed by private companies. For example, businesses are free to limit the speech of their employees and customers on their premises. However, in the 1980 case *Pruneyard Shopping Center v. Robins*, the Supreme Court found that when private property, such as a shopping mall,

Negative Effects

An October 2020 survey by the Pew Research Center found that 64 percent of US adults say social media is having a mostly negative effect on the way things are going in the United States. Only 10 percent say social media is having a mostly positive effect.

When asked why they think social media is having a negative effect on the country, most expressed concern about misinformation. Roughly three in ten (28 percent) of the respondents who hold a negative view of social media mention the spread of misinformation. "False information is spread at lightning speed—and false information never seems to go away," commented a seventy-one-year-old woman.

Younger adults have a more positive view of social media than older adults do. Fifteen percent of those ages eighteen to twenty-nine believe social media is having a mostly positive effect on the way things are going. Some, however, readily acknowledge the problems. "Social media is rampant with misinformation both about the coronavirus and political and social issues, and the social media organizations do not do enough to combat this," observed a twenty-six-year-old woman.

Quoted in Brooke Auxier, "64% of Americans Say Social Media Have a Mostly Negative Effect on the Way Things Are Going in the U.S. Today," Pew Research Center, October 15, 2020. www.pew research.org.

functions as a public forum, the business cannot bar the exercise of free speech. In 1995 the Supreme Court applied this logic to privately owned electronic networks, such as cable television channels, finding that they, too, are public forums and thus are governed by the First Amendment. In such situations, private companies must permit a free exchange of ideas.

In 2017 the Supreme Court expanded this concept to include social media. In *Packingham v. North Carolina*, the Supreme Court ruled that social networking websites like Instagram and Facebook are public forums in which speech is protected from government interference. "While in the past there may have been difficulty in identifying the most important places (in a spatial sense) for the exchange of views, today the answer is clear. It is cyberspace—the 'vast democratic forums of the Internet' in general, and social media in particular,"[13] wrote Justice Anthony Kennedy for the majority.

In *Packingham*, the court said the government cannot bar people from participating in social media as part of a criminal sentence. While *Packingham* applied to state action, some legal scholars believe the public forum part of the ruling opens the door to First Amendment claims. In 2017 Prager University sued YouTube on exactly these grounds, claiming that the world's largest social media platform had violated the school's First Amendment rights by flagging some of its videos as "inappropriate." A federal court in California ruled in YouTube's favor, finding that private companies are not bound by the First Amendment. Prager University lost an appeal in the Ninth Circuit Court in 2020 but planned to take its case to the Supreme Court.

Some free speech advocates believe that flagging, screening, and deleting social media posts violates the spirit of free speech, if not the law. "I think there's Republican and Democrat concern about the power that's being used by social media outlets to tell us what we can see and what we can't, what's true and what's not,"[14] said South Carolina senator Lindsay Graham at the Senate hearing that Zuckerberg and Dorsey attended in November 2020.

The social media moguls did not back down from their positions. Zuckerberg said:

> Sometimes the right thing to do from a safety or security perspective isn't the best for privacy or free expression, so we have to choose what we believe is best for our community and for the world. Making these tradeoffs is not straightforward, and whatever path we choose, inevitably some people are disappointed. In addition, people have very different ideas about how the internet should be governed. This is something many platforms struggle with, and it's why I believe we should resolve some of these tensions together as a society and in a way that people feel is legitimate.[15]

The debate about what is true, what is false, and who decides which is which will remain a major social issue for years to come.

Chapter Two

Forum for Hate

Shortly after 10:30 a.m. on August 3, 2019, a twenty-one-year-old White male dressed in dark clothing, wearing earmuff-style hearing protection, and armed with a semiautomatic rifle approached a Walmart in El Paso, Texas. While still in the parking lot, the man raised his rifle and began shooting the Saturday morning shoppers. He then entered the store and continued his rampage. When it was over, twenty-two people were dead and twenty-six were injured.

Witnesses said that the shooter, Patrick Crusius, did not fire his weapon indiscriminately. Instead, he targeted those who appeared to be Hispanic. After surrendering to police, Crusius told investigators that he had wanted to shoot as many Mexicans as he could. Why Mexicans? In a four-page racist manifesto he posted on the online message board 8chan shortly before the shooting, Crusius said that the mass shooting was "a response to the Hispanic invasion of Texas" and the "ethnic displacement"[16] of Whites.

Motivated by Hate

Crusius also said he was roused to action by the writings and actions of Brenton Tarrant. On March 15, 2019, Tarrant opened fire inside two mosques in Christchurch, New Zealand. He killed fifty-one people and injured forty. Tarrant, age twenty-eight, broadcast the first of his two shooting rampages on Facebook Live. He also posted a seventy-four-page manifesto on 8chan calling for White men of European heritage to stop the "Great Replacement," a White supremacist conspiracy theory that claims people of European descent are being overwhelmed by Middle Eastern refugees in Europe and by Hispanics in the United States. Tarrant himself was moved to action by a 1,516-page manifesto by Norwegian White supremacist Anders Behring Breivik. Breivik killed seventy-seven people, including many children, in a 2011 rampage, using guns and bombs. Breivik emailed his manifesto to one thousand people, and it has been circulating on racist websites and on social media ever since.

Crusius's, Tarrant's, and Breivik's manifestos are examples of hate speech. The *Oxford English Dictionary* defines hate speech as "abusive or threatening speech or writing that expresses prejudice against a particular group, especially on the basis of race, religion, or sexual orientation."[17] The Convention on Cybercrime of the Council of Europe, known as the Budapest Convention, which serves as a guideline for any country developing laws against cybercrime, defines hate speech as "all forms of expression which spread, incite, promote or justify racial hatred, xenophobia, anti-Semitism or other forms of hatred based on intolerance, including intolerance expressed by aggressive nationalism and ethnocentrism, discrimination and hostility against minorities, migrants and people of immigrant origin."[18]

A Surge in Hate Speech

Because of the internet and social media, more hate speech is being read by more people now than at any time since the government of Nazi Germany flooded Europe with anti-Semitic and White supremacist propaganda in the 1930s and early 1940s. According to the Southern Poverty Law Center (SPLC), a nonprofit civil rights organization, there were 940 hate groups in the United States in 2019, an increase of 20 percent since 2014. These groups vilify not only Jews and people of color but also the LGBTQ community. In fact, the SPLC reports that groups that target LGBTQ individuals represented the fastest-growing sector

Mourners visit a memorial in El Paso, Texas, to remember the twenty-two people killed during a shooting rampage at a Walmart in August 2019.

among hate groups in 2019—increasing from 49 groups in 2018 to 70 in 2019, a 43 percent increase. About one-fourth of all hate groups—255 in 2019—are Black separatists, who typically hold views that are anti-Semitic, anti-LGBTQ and anti-White.

While many hate groups hold in-person meetings, most of their activity occurs online. The Simon Wiesenthal Center, a global human rights organization, has found about fifteen thousand websites, social media pages, and online forums that are dedicated to inciting hatred based on ethnicity, race, or sexual preference. Hate speech on official websites is only part of the problem—perhaps the lesser part. Hate speech also occurs in individual posts by social media users on YouTube, Facebook, and Twitter, as well as in Yahoo! and Google groups. From January to March 2020, Facebook identified 9.6 million hate speech posts, an increase of 68 percent over the last three months of 2019. The company said that 4.7 million of these posts came from organized hate groups, but 4.9 million came from individual users. And the number is growing at an alarming rate. Facebook says that the number of hate speech posts for the first quarter of 2020 represented a sixfold increase since the second half of 2017, the earliest point for which data is available.

Hate Speech Harms

With online hate speech on the rise, experts wonder what effects it has on offline attitudes and behaviors. In 2019 two New York University researchers conducted a study to see whether there is a correlation between online hate speech and physical hate crimes. Using artificial intelligence, they analyzed 532 million tweets in one hundred cities across the United States. The researchers found that cities with the greatest number of targeted, hateful tweets also had the highest number of hate crimes. "Overall, our findings suggest that race/ethnicity-based online discrimination was associated with an increase in race/ethnicity-based hate crimes," the researchers write. "Our results provide a critical piece of information to the ongoing conversation related to how online discrimination could translate to the physical world."[19]

Social media hate speech causes mental harm even when it does not lead to physical violence. "The victims of hateful speech experience psychological symptoms, similar to post-traumatic stress disorder, such as pain, fear, anxiety, nightmares, and intrusive thoughts of intimidation and denigration," write researchers at the Georgia Institute of Technology. The researchers authored a 2020 study that looked at 6 million Reddit comments shared in 174 college communities. They found that 25 percent of these groups had more hate speech than noncollege Reddit groups. "We also find that the exposure to hate leads to greater stress expression [in comments on Reddit]," write the researchers. "Prejudice, discrimination, intolerance, and hatred can

> "Overall, our findings suggest that race/ethnicity-based online discrimination was associated with an increase in race/ethnicity-based hate crimes."[19]
>
> —New York University researchers

lead to stress and lowered self-esteem among minorities in college campuses, even if they are not the direct victims of specific events."[20]

Hate speech can intimidate people into silence. In fact, that is one of the goals of those who spread hate speech. A 2016 study by researchers at Carnegie Mellon University found that users of anonymous social media apps like Whisper and Yik Yak will leave the platforms if they are victims of hate speech. People can be made so uncomfortable by hate speech that they avoid any kind of civic discussion, according to Tarlach McGonagle, a senior researcher and lecturer at the University of Amsterdam. "All hate speech is problematic in so far as it targets individuals and has real consequences for them," writes McGonagle. "Various studies have shown that the harms caused by hate speech can take diverse forms: for instance, you can have psychological harm which affects people's self-confidence and self-esteem and perhaps their ability to participate freely in public debate and public affairs generally."[21]

Feeding Prejudice

Hate speech affects not only targeted individuals and groups but also bystanders from the speaker's own group. Exposure to hate speech can make people less sensitive to and less appalled by its threatening nature. As familiarity with hate speech grows, its underlying message can be absorbed by more people, leading to an increase in prejudice against the hate speech victims.

In a 2018 study published in the psychology journal *Aggressive Behavior*, researchers at the University of Warsaw in Poland tried to measure how hate speech increases prejudice. The researchers conducted two nationwide surveys and a controlled experiment that involved seventy-three volunteers. The researchers found that "frequent and repetitive exposure to hate speech leads to desensitization to this form of verbal violence and subsequently to lower evaluations of the victims and greater distancing, thus increasing outgroup prejudice."[22] The increased prejudice against the victims of hate speech makes it more likely that people who were bystanders will begin to engage in hate speech as well, thus spreading the social disease.

Hate-Spreading Bots

Knowing that hate speech is socially contagious, those who want to sow discord and deepen racial and political divisions often amplify their hate speech using fake accounts and software applications known as social bots. Social bots are similar to chatbots. Many companies use chatbots to provide automated customer service online, answering simple questions from customers via text chat. Like chatbots, social bots can simulate the way a person might

Twitter's Policy on Hateful Conduct

On December 2, 2020, Twitter updated its rules on hateful conduct to ban speech that dehumanizes people on the basis of race, ethnicity, or national origin. In March 2020 the company said it would ban abusive speech based on age, disability, and disease. The company's hateful conduct policy reads in part:

Hateful conduct: You may not promote violence against or directly attack or threaten other people on the basis of race, ethnicity, national origin, caste, sexual orientation, gender, gender identity, religious affiliation, age, disability, or serious disease. We also do not allow accounts whose primary purpose is inciting harm towards others on the basis of these categories.

Hateful imagery and display names: You may not use hateful images or symbols in your profile image or profile header. You also may not use your username, display name, or profile bio to engage in abusive behavior, such as targeted harassment or expressing hate towards a person, group, or protected category.

Twitter, "Hateful Conduct Policy," 2021. https://help.twitter.com.

respond to online comments. However, social bots are more limited in their conversations than chatbots. Their messages are very simple and often are written by the people using them to spread their hate speech. Nevertheless, social bots can reply to thousands of social media posts and comments in minutes, spreading hate speech at an alarming rate. A 2020 study by researchers at Carnegie Mellon University found that about 40 percent of all messages about the COVID-19 pandemic were generated by social bots.

A separate Carnegie Mellon University study found that social bots were used to spread hate speech and sow political discord on Twitter related to the COVID-19 pandemic. During a seventy-five-day period from March 5 to May 19, 2020, the researchers found that 3 million comments—about 15 percent of the total—were made by social bots. "This points to more concerted attempts by inauthentic accounts to heighten politically charged conflicts amid the pandemic,"[23] write the researchers.

Social bots can reply to thousands of social media posts in minutes, spreading hate speech at an alarming rate. A 2020 study found that about 40 percent of all messages about the COVID-19 pandemic were generated by social bots.

Instagram Troll Targets Asian American

The COVID-19 pandemic has seen a rise in hate speech directed at Asian Americans. Eric Chan, who owns the Jade Garden restaurant in Seattle, is one of those who was targeted with racist remarks in May 2020. "It was on my public Instagram profile," Chan explains, "telling me to cook my dog and eat it for Chow Mein."

Chan described the incident in his own post, and the Instagram troll retaliated. "He found out that I exposed him for being a racist on my profile," says Chan. "This guy photoshopped my handle name onto a fake image, and it has me spewing out these racist tirades, you know, black lives don't matter." The fake message was then shared on a neighborhood Facebook page. "So now," says Chan, "I'm getting death threats at the restaurant. People are calling and saying I'm a racist."

A week after the online rumor appeared, the restaurant was vandalized and burglarized. A few days later, Jade Garden was damaged during protests over the death of George Floyd. Chan believes the restaurant was targeted because of the online rumors. Chan pleaded for the attacks to stop. "We're just trying to work, Man," he said.

Quoted in Natalie Swaby, "Seattle Man Receives Death Threats After Racist Attack Online," King5 News, May 25, 2020. www.king5.com.

Combating Hate

Social media companies are using their own automated systems to combat hate speech, as they do with false and misleading information. Twitter says that in 2020 its content moderation software identified and removed more than 50 percent of abusive tweets before they were reported by users. "We create our rules to keep people safe on Twitter, and they continuously evolve to reflect the realities of the world we operate within," states the company's blog. "Our primary focus is on addressing the risks of offline harm, and research shows that dehumanizing language increases that risk."[24] Facebook says its policing software removed 9.6 million hate speech posts in the first three months of 2020.

Nevertheless, some computing experts are skeptical that technology can solve the problem. "Many excellent methods will be developed to improve the information environment, but the history of online systems shows that bad actors can and will always find ways around them,"[25] says Paul N. Edwards, William J. Perry Fellow in International Security at Stanford University. For example, those who want to post hate speech can open fake accounts, send out a barrage of hateful messages, and close the accounts before the speech moderators even notice them. They can also gain access to existing accounts without permission, a process known as hacking, and use the legitimate account to spread hateful messages.

The continued prevalence of hate speech contradicts the notion that good speech will overcome bad speech in a free marketplace of ideas. Since the defeat of the racist regime of Nazi Germany in 1945, the evils of hate speech have been discussed in countless books, articles, classrooms, churches, and websites and on social media. This good speech—no matter how true and no matter how powerful—has failed to drive hate speech out of the marketplace of ideas. Hate speech persists because something about it appeals to the dark side of human nature. Hate speech creates real psychological harm in its victims and dehumanizes people to the point that others feel justified in committing real violence against them. For these and other reasons, it will continue to be banned by social media companies so that its dangers can be minimized as much as humanly possible.

Chapter Three

Cyberbullying and Shaming

Ten-year-old Marian Hernández Rojas, a fifth-grader in Mesa, Arizona, loved to smile and wear the bright colors of 1980s fashion. But Marian's cheerful demeanor hid a dark secret. She was being bullied on social media. Her pain was so great that in July 2020, a few days before her eleventh birthday, Marian took her own life. "She was always happy, but the more I dig, the more questions I ask, the more I found out she was deeply hurt inside," says Angel Rojas, Marian's twenty-three-year-old brother. "She was really good at hiding it."[26]

A Secret World

When Angel opened Marian's cell phone, he found that she had deleted all of her pictures and had blocked some-one on Instagram. Speaking with Marian's friends, Angel learned that his sister had been receiving messages from cyberbullies, including creepy messages from another Ins-tagram user. What that person said remains a mystery. "We will never know. It's something she took to the grave," says Angel. "If I could've seen what she was seeing, if I could've seen who she was talking to, she could've been with us. Unfortunately for us, we didn't take those 30 minutes, one hour, two hours."[27]

Marian's story illustrates one of the major problems with social media bullying and shaming—namely, that it often takes place away from the watchful eyes of teachers, parents, and other family members. Secrecy is one of the things that distinguishes cyberbullying from in-person bullying, which usually takes place at school or in another social situation where adults can become involved. "Smartphones provide children the first environment in history that exists without any oversight by any adult whatsoever," writes social critic Jonathon Van Maren. "The reason cyberbullying is so effective and so dangerous is the fact that social media has created an alternative world, inhabited by young people and their peers and inaccessible to parents and guardians."[28]

A Widespread Problem

Marian's cyberbullying experience is not uncommon. A 2018 Pew Research Center study found that 59 percent of US teens had experienced cyberbullying at some time in their lives. A 2019 study from the Cyberbullying Research Center found that 36 percent of US teens had been recently cyberbullied.

Instagram is the leading source of cyberbullying, according to the antibullying organization Ditch the Label. A 2017 survey of young adults found that 42 percent had experienced cyberbullying on Instagram, compared to 37 percent on Facebook and 31 percent on Snapchat. Only 9 percent reported having experienced cyberbullying on Twitter. The effects of cyberbullying can be devastating. A 2020 study by Ditch the Label found that 44 percent of those who had been bullied felt anxious, 36 percent felt depressed, and 33 percent had suicidal thoughts.

A Focus on Appearance

Cyberbullies mock people for many different reasons, but personal appearance is at the top of the list, according to Ditch the

Label's 2020 survey. Nearly half of the teens who had been bullied in the previous twelve months—47 percent—said that it was because of their appearance.

A Raleigh, North Carolina, teen named Ethan Cohen is one of those who felt the pain of online bullying that focused on his physical appearance. When Cohen was in middle school in 2014, an unidentified classmate began taking photographs of him without his knowledge and posting them on Instagram under the user name "ethan_cohens_neck_vein." The feed attracted people who mocked the appearance of a prominent muscle in Cohen's neck. One person likened it to the Great Wall of China. Another said its size could only be determined by "systems of equations."[29] Cohen tried to laugh off the demeaning posts as a harmless prank, but he also reported them to Instagram for violating the platform's guidelines against negative physical descriptions. The company took no action.

Abbigale Phillips, a sixteen-year-old student at Sachse High School in Sachse, Texas, was also mocked on Instagram for

Experts believe one reason cyberbullying is dangerous is that social media has created a private platform for young people with little to no supervision by parents and guardians.

her appearance. In 2017, when Phillips was in seventh grade, a classmate ridiculed her hair and called her "the annoying red-head." The words wounded Phillips. "It made me not like myself," she remembers. "I felt if other people couldn't see my worth then maybe I didn't have any." Feeling sad and empty, Phillips attempted to take her own life. She survived, but the bullying continued. She attempted to take her life five more times over the next three years. Eventually, through counseling, she learned how to cope with the harassment. In 2020 she told a reporter, "I know how to properly handle my emotions. I actually have the skills to . . . not harp on the negative things."[30]

Physical appearance is just one of many things bullies mock on social media. According to Ditch the Label, 30 percent of those who were bullied in the twelve months before the survey was conducted said they were targeted because of their interests

A Fourteen-Year-Old Cyberbullying Victim Speaks Out

Teens Against Bullying is a website where middle and high school students can find ways to address bullying. Students are encouraged to tell their stories as a way to be heard and to help others understand bullying. In February 2021, an anonymous teen posted this story:

i am 14 years old and i had gone to an elementary-middle school since the 5th grade. It is a fairly small school and there was only 36 kids in my grade. From 5th-8th i was loved and treasured and had so many friends, that was until corona hit. During the [Black Lives Matter] protests many of them made racist jokes and i called them out on it. Since then my number and instagram has been leaked on social media, ive lost every single friend, i have become a shell of who i used to be and i am downright miserable. it got better for a while but they still talk about me almost a year later, i dont think anyone realizes the effects of cyberbullying until it happens to them.

Anonymous, "My Bullying Story," Teens Against Bullying, February 1, 2021. https://pacerteens againstbullying.org.

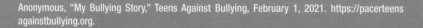

or hobbies; 24 percent were targeted because of something they did; and 22 percent were called gay or lesbian when they were not. Other common themes of social media mockery included grades (both high and low), mannerisms, low household income, a health condition or disability, and race. In addition to being cyberbullied for his physical appearance, Cohen is one of those who was taunted for his sexuality. When he came out as gay in high school, a popular student called him a "faggot" and "failed abortion"[31] on Instagram.

No Escape

There have always been bullies, of course, but social media makes bullying easier. A bully does not have to wait for an opportune time—passing periods, lunch hours, or before or after school—to strike. Social media gives a bully around-the-clock access to potential victims. This not only strengthens the hand of bullies, it also increases the torment of victims, who often feel like there is no escape from the harassment. "A generation ago, the bullying would stop when you got home from school," writes Van Maren. "Today, you can be bullied at home, in your bedroom."[32] Yael, a fifteen-year-old Instagram user, describes how she could never escape the taunts of a friend turned bully:

> She unfollowed me, blocked me, unblocked me, then messaged me days on end, paragraphs. She posted about me constantly on her account, mentioned me in her Story, and messaged me over and over again for weeks. . . . Every time I logged on to my account, I didn't want to be there. I knew when I opened the app, she would be there. I was having a lot of anxiety over it, a lot of stress.[33]

Social media also gives a bully a larger audience for the humiliation. A shaming comment in a hallway at school might be heard by a small number of classmates and repeated to more, but a degrading post on social media can be seen by hundreds and, if it goes viral, by thousands, increasing the trauma for the victim. John Trautwein of Duluth, Georgia, is convinced that this is what happened to his son Will. Will killed himself at age fifteen. His father believes that social media contributed to Will's difficulties. "Every single mistake that Will ever made, there was a fear that it would be on YouTube, on Snapchat, on Facebook," says John. "They know that if they mess up, everyone will know about it by lunchtime."[34] Public embarrassment is especially painful for teens, who have not fully developed defenses against shaming and whose emerging identities may be somewhat fragile.

Hiding Behind the Screen

Perhaps worst of all, social media allows bullies to hide their identities with fake screen names and fake social media accounts. Anonymity makes people feel bolder. "In real-life bullying, you know what's doing it," says Skye (not her real name), a fourteen-year-old Instagram user who spoke with the media using a pseudonym. "Hate pages could be anyone. It could be someone you know, someone you don't know—you don't know what you know, and it's scary because it's really out of control at that point. Teachers tell you with bullying [to] just say 'Stop,' but in this case you can't, and you don't even know who to tell stop to."[35]

Ethan Cohen, now eighteen, says that the most disturbing aspect of his cyberbullying was the not knowing who was doing it. "The anonymity of it was freaky,"[36] he says. It made him suspicious of everyone around him, eroding trust and causing him to feel even more isolated. Anonymity also means the bullies are less likely to be held accountable for their actions. Parents, teachers, and counselors who might intervene with a physical-world bully can do little to stop

> "Hate pages could be anyone. It could be someone you know, someone you don't know. . . . Teachers tell you with bullying [to] just say 'Stop,' but in this case you can't, and you don't even know who to tell stop to."[35]
>
> —Skye, a fourteen-year-old Instagram user

the nameless, faceless tormentor. All they can do is counsel the victim to avoid the harmful posts or leave the platform altogether.

For many teens, quitting the platform is not really a solution. They believe the bully will continue posting about them, and they worry about what will be said in their absence. "You know someone's talking about you, they're posting about you, they're messaging about you,"[37] Yael explains. She says she would rather know what the bully is saying than to imagine something even worse.

False Comparisons

Sometimes social media shaming is not the result of bullying. Sometimes it results from comparing oneself to the often-unrealistic images of happiness, success, and attractiveness

"You know someone's talking about you, they're posting about you, they're messaging about you."[37]

—Yael, a fifteen-year-old Instagram user

that others present on social media. Jamie Zelazny, an assistant professor at the University of Pittsburgh School of Medicine, is conducting a study to assess the impact of social media on suicidal teens. In 2020 Zelazny and her colleagues found that 67 percent of participants in a program for suicidal teens reported feeling worse about their own lives because of social media.

Many of the bad feelings came from comparing themselves to others. Seventy-three percent felt they needed to improve their appearance online, and 60 percent believed they needed to post content that drew likes and approval from others. The pressure to compete can be unbearable. Lacey Morgan, a twenty-six-year-old native of Pocatello, Idaho, sees a large and destructive schism between a person's awareness of their own faults and the

Self-Shaming

Shaming sometimes occurs when individuals compare themselves unfavorably to others—something that Facebook's constant feed of others' photos and accomplishments makes almost unavoidable. Teens in particular are vulnerable to self-shaming. Scientific studies have found connections between the amount of time spent on social media and various mental health issues. One found that Facebook users under age eighteen who spent more time on Facebook were more likely to exhibit negative states such as envy and insecurity. Another found that those who use social media a lot had more body image concerns and eating disorders. The effects can be immediate. A study conducted in the United Kingdom and Australia found that "female participants reported more negative mood after just 10 minutes of browsing their Facebook account compared with those who browsed an appearance-neutral control website." In fact, more participants who spent time on Facebook said they wanted to change their appearance than did those who visited the control website.

Elia Abi-Jaoude et al., "Smartphones, Social Media Use and Youth Mental Health," *Canadian Medical Association Journal*, February 10, 2020. www.ncbi.nlm.nih.gov.

constant stream of success stories that they see in social media. "We have our blooper reel in our head, and everyone else's highlight reel in the palm of our hands,"[38] Morgan says.

Taking Steps Against Bullying

All social media platforms have user policies that forbid bullying, shaming, and harassment, but enforcing these policies can be difficult. Part of the problem is the sheer number of users. Facebook has 2.9 billion monthly active users worldwide; YouTube, 2 billion; Instagram, 1 billion; and Twitter, 330 million.

Because of these vast numbers of users, social media companies police their platforms with both human and computerized content reviewers. Facebook pioneered automatic content moderation with an AI program known as Deep Text, which is capable of analyzing several thousand posts and comments per second. Instagram, which is owned by Facebook, also uses Deep Text to moderate content. YouTube, which is owned by Google, has its own AI monitoring systems.

Automated systems can be highly efficient. YouTube reported that from April to June 2020, its automated filter removed 11 million videos that violated the company's guidelines. "Over 50 percent of those 11 million videos were removed without a single view by an actual YouTube user and over 80 percent were removed with less than 10 views," says YouTube's chief product officer, Neal Mohan. "And so that's the power of machines."[39]

Facebook and Instagram initially targeted unwanted promotional posts and comments, known as spam. They then broadened Deep Text's mission to eliminate hate speech. Bullying and shaming is the last frontier of content moderation. Harassment can be more difficult to identify than hate speech, which usually contains words that are easily flagged, such as racial slurs. Bullying and shaming can be much more subtle, employing techniques such as sarcasm, in which one thing is said but its opposite is meant. For example, a person might comment on an embarrassing or less-than-perfect photograph with the words "You look

One problem of policing harassment on social media platforms is the sheer number of users. Facebook, YouTube, Instagram, and Twitter have billions of users globally.

awesome!" when the bully really means the person does not look awesome. Other times the comment is sincere but unwelcome. A person might comment "You look awesome" on every photo another person posts, causing the person posting the pictures to feel they are being watched and even stalked by a stranger. Such comments might trigger the AI programs to analyze things like whether both people leave comments on each other's pictures or whether they tag each other. If so, the people likely are friends, but if not, the comments might be suspicious. Other factors the AI systems look at is whether one person has blocked the other or whether someone with a similar account name has been banned from the platform.

To help users stop shaming before it starts, Instagram created a tool called Restrict. It allows a user to identify a bully without that person knowing it. Every time the bully makes a comment on a user's post, the user sees it before it is available for everyone to see. The user can allow the comment, delete it, or leave it pending—all without notifying the bully. If the comment is pending, the bully can see it, but no one else can. Teens in particular like this feature because it allows them to silence a bully without blocking him or her. Unlike blocking, restricting prevents the bully from knowing the victim has been hurt, and it allows the victim to continue monitoring what the bully is doing.

Negative Images

Some bullying does not involve words at all. For example, an ex-boyfriend or ex-girlfriend might simply tag an ex in a photo that shows him or her with someone new. Or someone might tag everyone in a photo but leave out one person on purpose, so that person feels excluded. Sometimes a person will take a screen shot of another person's photo and then alter it so it is embarrassing. "Teens are exceptionally creative,"[40] says Instagram head of public policy Karina Newton.

The manipulation of photos is difficult for AI systems to identify, but social media engineers are using a technique known as machine learning to improve their ability to identify the hurtful ones. The engineers have learned that side-by-side, split-screen images often are demeaning, especially if one side shows a person and the other side shows an animal. A photo with an X drawn on the image is also a red flag, suggesting that the targeted person does not belong in the photo. Yoav Shapira, a lead engineer at Instagram, is optimistic about the ability of technology to identify bullying images. "It's going to get much better,"[41] says Shapira.

Many experts say that better technical solutions are needed—and soon. Human nature is not going to change in the short run, and efforts to stop cyberbullying can only do so much. Each day that passes means more pain, more anxiety, and potentially, more deaths.

Chapter Four

Designed to Addict

"I am a recovering social media addict," writes Tracey Folly, a columnist and blogger. Folly says she avoided social media for years but eventually opened accounts on Facebook and Twitter. "Once I started using social media, I was hooked," she says. She remembers the rush of excitement she felt the first time people responded to her online presence. "I opened my first Twitter account, followed my first three celebrity accounts, and left the house to go grocery shopping," she remembers. "Without a smartphone, it wasn't until I returned home hours later that I discovered my follower count had swelled from zero to five. That was the moment I knew I'd find my tribe." She followed back the five Twitter accounts and began to exchange tweets with people from around the world. "I found myself basking in the feeling of popularity that I had only dreamed of in high school,"[42] she recalls.

Folly soon found that she was consumed by what was happening on social media. "During the height of my social media addiction, I paid as little attention as possible to people in their flesh and blood form. Instead, I buried my nose in my Amazon Kindle Fire tablet and kept refresh-refresh-refreshing Twitter and Facebook until someone had something new to say." Even though her tablet was not waterproof, she would take it in the shower to check her social media accounts. "That's how terrified I was that I would miss something," she says. "FOMO [fear of missing out] is real."[43] Her FOMO was so intense that she even checked her social media accounts while driving. She recalls those days, with a hint of sarcasm:

> Another fun way I fed my social media addiction was by keeping my tablet on the passenger seat of my car and searching for a free WiFi signal every time I arrived at a red light or stop sign just so I could check for new direct messages on Facebook and Twitter. If the signal was strong and traffic was light, I might even have the chance to eke out a quick message or two in the hopes that I would have a reply before I reached the next intersection or traffic signal. I told myself that I was being super safe. After all, no one ever got into a car accident due to using social media while driving. Right?[44]

Folly eventually recognized that her obsession with social media was out of control and even dangerous. She decided she would close her accounts "I wish I could say that I quit cold turkey, but I didn't," she recalls. "There were a few slips involved before I deleted all my social media accounts without accidentally on purpose reactivating them before it was too late. The important thing is that I did indeed get myself and my addictive personality away from social media for good. I have more important things to do."[45]

> "During the height of my social media addiction, I paid as little attention as possible to people in their flesh and blood form. Instead, I buried my nose in my Amazon Kindle Fire tablet and kept refresh-refresh-refreshing Twitter and Facebook until someone had something new to say."[43]
>
> —Tracey Folly, blogger and social media addict

Behavioral Addiction

Folly's all-consuming involvement with social media is considered by some psychologists to be a kind of addiction known as a behavioral addiction. Behavioral addiction is a mental health condition in which a person engages in a certain behavior even if that behavior

Social media can become a dangerous addiction. The addiction can be so intense that some users risk checking social media accounts even while driving, out of fear that they may miss a post.

causes him or her harm. The American Psychiatric Association does not recognize social media addiction in the fifth edition of the *Diagnostic and Statistical Manual of Mental Disorders*, but it does recognize several other behavioral addictions, including gambling disorder, eating disorders, and shopping addiction. Recognition of an addiction or disorder means, among other things, that medical insurance will help pay for its treatment.

Although social media addiction has not been formally recognized by the medical community, some psychologists believe it should be. One of those is Mark D. Griffiths, a professor of behavioral addiction and director of Nottingham Trent University's International Gaming Research Unit. He has written that those who engage heavily in social media may exhibit the six characteristics that make up behavior addiction. These include the following:

- salience, when a behavior becomes the most important part of a person's life

- mood modification, when a person uses a behavior to alter his or her moods or escape from problems
- tolerance, when a person has to spend more time engaged in a behavior to produce the same feelings of well-being
- conflict, when a behavior creates relationship problems or disrupts everyday life
- withdrawal symptoms, when a person has unpleasant feelings or physical sensations when not able to engage in a behavior
- relapse, when a person tries to curb or give up a behavior but reverts to excessive use

Griffiths believes that when social media overuse meets these six criteria, it is properly classified as a behavioral addiction.

A Growing Problem

Using a definition of addiction similar to Griffiths's, researchers at the University of Hong Kong estimate that 6 percent of the world's 4.5 billion internet users—about 270 million people—have some level of internet addiction. According to the *Digital 2020: Global Digital Overview* report by internet research firms We Are Social and Hootsuite, 84 percent of internet users, or 3.8 billion people worldwide, use social media. Many psychologists believe that the addiction rate among social media users is even higher than it is among general internet users. A survey published by Statista in 2021 found that 39 percent of US internet users reported feeling completely or somewhat addicted to social media. Nine percent of respondents said that the statement "I am addicted to social media" describes them "completely," while 30 percent said the statement describes them "somewhat."[46] With more than 246 million social media users in the United States, these percentages would mean that more than 22 million Americans feel they are completely addicted to social media, and another 73 million feel they are somewhat addicted.

The Effects of Social Media Addiction

Overuse of social media results in countless hours of wasted time, which can damage personal relationships and cause academic or work performance to decline. These conflicts contribute to mental health issues, including anxiety and loneliness. Researchers have found that using social media excessively creates mental conditions even apart from the obvious conflicts with people and school or work. The fear of missing out and the concern about whether the user's shared content is popular creates anxiety.

Heavy social media use has been linked to loneliness and depression. Researchers at the University of Pennsylvania studied 143 students, divided into two groups, for three weeks in 2018. Members of one group used social media as usual, while members of the other group limited their use to ten minutes per social media site per day. "What we found overall is that if you use less social media, you are actually less depressed and less lonely, meaning that the decreased social media use is what causes that qualitative shift in your well-being,"[47] says Jordyn Young, one of the paper's coauthors.

Heavy social media use has been linked to loneliness and depression. Studies have found that a reduction in social media use improves well-being.

Facing Social Media Addiction

Writing for *Psychology Today*, Dana Bowman describes how she recognized that she was addicted to social media and why:

> Every night I found myself scrolling through endless videos of people who were on the hunt for just the right sequined shoe for their Zara dress, or of dogs finding the right owner to free them from death row, or someone making a chocolate torte so lovingly that it was basically erotica. I loved it. . . . It latched onto me and I just kept scrolling. And scrolling.
>
> And scrolling. . . .
>
> Social media changes the brain. It can trigger a dopamine hit, which ultimately is unable to be filled. It can engender chronic distraction, wreaking havoc on our peace, our self-control, our priorities. . . .
>
> I realized that social media was feeding a deeper addiction: my need for certainty. We all want clear answers to how our lives play out, but in my case, my constant scrolling was like trying to find spiritual direction from a Zoltar the Mind Reader carnival game. My anxiety would only increase, as the constant pendulum of ideas and opinions made me dizzy and sad. And empty.

Dana Bowman, "My Name Is Dana, and I'm Addicted to Mindless Scrolling," *Highly Functioning Is Highly Dangerous* (blog), *Psychology Today*, September 6, 2020. www.psychologytoday.com.

The mental upheaval caused by heavy social media use also impairs decision-making, according to a 2019 study by researchers at Michigan State University (MSU). The researchers first measured how involved the study's subjects were with social media. The subjects with the deepest emotional involvement performed the worst on a decision-making test often used in this type of research. "In particular, our results indicate that excessive users [of social networking sites] may make more risky decisions,"[48] write the researchers.

The MSU researchers were struck by the similarity between the performance of social media addicts and those who abused drugs, such as cocaine or heroin. Previous studies showed that those with substance abuse disorders tended to "fail to learn from their mistakes and continue down a path of negative outcomes,"[49] according to Dar Meshi, an assistant professor in MSU's neuroscience program and leader of the decision-making study. The same was true of those who overuse social media. "Our research supports a parallel between individuals displaying problematic, excessive social media use and individuals with substance use disorders,"[50] Meshi explains.

The Chemical Link

Social media addiction is similar to substance abuse in another way: both are driven by changes in brain chemistry. Using social media can cause the nervous system to release natural chemicals in the brain that create pleasurable feelings, just as cocaine and amphetamines do. These pleasant sensations can become addictive. In the case of social media, scientists believe that positive reactions to shared content, including "likes," comments, and shares, cause the brain to release a chemical known as dopamine. This chemical is a neurotransmitter, which the nervous system uses to send messages between nerve cells. Dopamine is part of what is known as the reward circuit, meaning it is normally released to reward behaviors that are vital to survival, such as eating, drinking, socializing, and having sex. However, the release of dopamine can be caused by any achievement or success, from solving a puzzle to receiving positive feedback on social media. For some people, the desire to receive these natural rewards can become an irresistible craving.

Dopamine also plays a role in the formation of memories. It causes changes in the brain's neural network, reinforcing the connection between the activity and the pleasant experience. This memory encourages the person to automatically repeat the activity, turning it into a kind of habit. These dopamine-made memories are one reason why many people routinely pick up their phones and begin scrolling through social media without really thinking about what they are doing.

Manipulating Brain Chemistry

Certain industries—including entertainment, advertising, and gambling—are based on an understanding of the brain's inner workings. The goal is to create experiences that stimulate the

A Blogger Tells How She Ended Her Social Media Addiction

Kaylin, a blogger, considers herself addicted to social media. She offers tips on breaking the social media habit:

> I'm addicted to social media. It really has highlighted my insecurities and probably has made new ones. The problem is that social media lets us present the best parts of ourselves and fully promotes our tendency for comparison. You may also be like me and say I'll check it real quick, but that check turns in to multiple checks throughout the day or sometimes an hour passes by and you've just been mindlessly scrolling.
>
> Breaking an addiction means forming new habits to replace it.
>
> Track your hours (so you can be shocked how much time you spend on your phone)
>
> Create time limits (the iPhone lets you make screen limits on your phone from the settings.)
>
> Find hobbies to replace the scroll time or put the phone down and do those tasks you've been avoiding. (They aren't going to go away.)
>
> Make goals and actually break them down to start working on them today!
>
> My approach . . . in breaking the addiction is all of the above but also . . . having specific time "blocks" for certain tasks and responsibilities.

Kaylin, "Breaking My Social Media Addiction," *My Life as Kaylin* (blog), July 21, 2020. https://my-lifeaskaylin.com.

reward circuit to release dopamine, creating pleasant associations with their product or service. For example, a slot machine's flashing lights, chiming bells, and clattering coins can stimulate the release of neurotransmitters in a gambler's brain. This creates a surge of pleasure and well-being. The manipulation of the brain's reward circuit can keep a gambler transfixed for hours at a time, typically resulting in much larger profits for the gaming establishment than if the player stopped after an hour or so.

Like casinos, social media companies make money by keeping their users involved with their products for long periods of time—the longer the better. The companies charge advertisers money based on how many people in a target audience are exposed to the advertiser's message. These advertising exposures are known as "impressions." The longer a user is engaged with social media, the more impressions that person receives, and the more money the company can make. "You have a business model designed to engage you and get you to basically suck as much time out of your life as possible and then selling that attention to advertisers,"[51] observes former Facebook engineer Sandy Parakilas.

> "You have a business model designed to engage you and get you to basically suck as much time out of your life as possible and then selling that attention to advertisers."[51]
>
> —Sandy Parakilas, former Facebook engineer

To keep people engaged, social media sites incorporate features that trigger the user's reward circuit. "They can't force a needle into our arms to inject us with dopamine, so they trick our brains to produce it,"[52] observes Kareem Darwish, a scientist at Qatar Computing Research Institute. The social media site does this by sending the user a steady stream of notifications about likes, loves, and shares. Former Facebook engineer Justin Rosenstein calls these alerts "bright dings of pseudo-pleasure"[53] because they stimulate the release of dopamine, creating feelings of well-being.

The design model being used in social media has proved to be highly effective. "It's as if they're taking behavioral cocaine and just sprinkling it all over your interface," says Aza Raskin, a software engineer who designed the feature that enables users to continuously scroll through a social media feed. "And that's the thing that keeps you like coming back and back and back." Raskin says that social media engineers are constantly designing new features to lure users into ever longer engagements with the platform. "Behind every screen on your phone, there are generally like literally a thousand (user experience) engineers that have worked on this thing to try to make it maximally addicting."[54]

> "It's as if they're taking behavioral cocaine and just sprinkling it all over your interface. And that's the thing that keeps you like coming back and back and back."[54]
>
> —Aza Raskin, a software engineer

Building in Uncertainty

One of the techniques that social media engineers use to increase engagement is unpredictability. Scientists know that the brain does not release dopamine every time a person succeeds at something. If it did, people would constantly feel contented, and that might prevent them from pursuing further challenges essential to survival. Instead, the brain releases dopamine only when an achievement follows a period of uncertainty, as when a slot machine player wins some coins after a long wait. The unpredictability of the outcome is part of what makes gambling so alluring.

Knowing this, social media engineers have built uncertainty into their platforms in the form of what are known as intermittent variable rewards. A user who posts a comment, picture, or video on social media does not know what reaction, if any, the item will receive. Not knowing the outcome helps trigger the release of dopamine when the user finally receives positive feedback. The uncertainty also fuels the anticipation the user feels. "Social media sites are chock-a-block with unpredictable rewards," says Mark D. Griffiths. "They are trying to grab users' attentions . . . to make social media users create a routine and habitually check their screens."[55] For some social media users, the cycle of posting, uncertainty, anticipation, and rewards is addicting.

Addressing the Problem

With evidence mounting that social media is addictive by design, Twitter CEO Jack Dorsey admitted to members of a congressional committee that social media platforms can be addictive. Testifying before the Senate Judiciary Committee in November 2020, Dorsey was asked by Senator Lindsey Graham if platforms like Twitter had the ability to become addicting. "I do think, like anything else, these tools can be addictive," said Dorsey. "And we should be aware of that, acknowledge it, and make sure that we are making our customers aware of better patterns of usage. The more information the better here."[56]

Facebook CEO Mark Zuckerberg also testified at the hearing. He rejected the notion that social media is addictive but said his company was working on ways to help customers curb their usage. "From what I've seen so far, it's inconclusive and most of the research suggests that the vast majority of people do not perceive or experience these services as addictive or have issues," Zuckerberg said. "But I do think that there should be controls given to people to help them manage their experience better and this is something that we're very focused on."[57]

Tristan Harris, a former Google employee and an advocate for more humane technology, does not believe that more information or simple controls will stop the craving for "the next dopamine fix." Harris says, "If the person is feeling the kind of anxiety and novelty-seeking craving in their lower nervous system that causes them to reach for their phone the second time this last 60 seconds, it's not because they just need a seat belt or . . . [need] a limit that says, 'don't do that.'"[58] Doubtful that social media giants will reform themselves, some social media critics believe that

For some people with addiction to social media, treatment is often the only way back to a healthy lifestyle. Family counseling can be beneficial as it teaches the user and parent or guardian about coping mechanisms.

the government should ban technologies that feed social media addiction. In 2019 Senator Josh Hawley of Missouri sponsored a bill designed to "prohibit social media companies from using practices that exploit human psychology or brain physiology to substantially impede freedom of choice, to require social media companies to take measures to mitigate the risks of internet addiction and psychological exploitation, and for other purposes."[59] The bill calls for social media companies to create stopping points in their feeds to prevent endless scrolling. It also calls for the elimination of autoplay, the function that automatically plays videos and music. The bill requires social media companies to provide a tool to allow users to see how much time they are spending on social media and to automatically cut off their social media feed when they reach their self-imposed limits. The bill was referred to committee for further study.

Modifying Behavior

Such measures might prevent some users from becoming addicted to social media, but for those who are already addicted, treatment is often the only way back to a healthy lifestyle. One-on-one counseling, group therapy, and family therapy are now available for people with social media addiction. Unlike treatment for substance addictions, which require addicts to give up intoxicating substances completely, treatment of behavioral addictions usually aims at modifying rather than eliminating the behavior. This is because behavioral addictions often involve activities people must engage in, including eating, shopping, and even internet use. One of the most successful behavioral addiction treatments is known as cognitive behavioral therapy. This therapy focuses on the thought processes, or cognition, that lead to the addictive behavior. The patient learns to identify the thoughts that trigger the behavior and then pause before acting on them. The patient learns strategies to challenge and overcome the addiction-related thoughts, thus stopping the addictive behavior before it starts.

Most of these treatment services are available on an outpatient basis, meaning the person with the problem lives at home and attends therapy sessions. In extreme cases, the person with the addiction might need to enter a residential treatment center. This is a place where the addicted person can live with others struggling with the same problem in an environment where the addictive substance or technology is not available. Isolating the patient from everyday life helps break patterns of addiction. The presence of others who share the problem helps patients face up to their addiction and learn ways to cope with it.

Introduction: Dangerous Words

1. Quoted in Paige St. John, "San Diego Veteran's Radical Path Led to Trump, QAnon and a Deadly Insurrection," *Los Angeles Times*, January 8, 2021. www.latimes.com.
2. Twitter Inc., "Permanent Suspension of @realDonaldTrump," *Twitter Blog*, January 8, 2021. https://blog.twitter.com.

Chapter One: Tearing at the Fabric of Society

3. Quoted in Jack Goodman and Flora Carmichael, "Covid-19: What's the Harm of 'Funny' Anti-vaccine Memes?," BBC, November 29, 2020. www.bbc.com.
4. Carrie Madej, *Urgent Information on COVID Vacc!ne*, BitChute, August 24, 2020. www.bitchute.com.
5. Quoted in Janna Anderson and Lee Rainie, "The Future of Truth and Misinformation Online," Pew Research Center, October 19, 2017. www.pewresearch.org.
6. Quoted in Richard Gray, "Lies, Propaganda and Fake News: A Challenge for Our Age," BBC, March 1, 2017. www.bbc.com.
7. Quoted in Mike Fendt, "Let's read line 17 out together," Facebook, December 25, 2020. www.facebook.com/mikefendt1/posts/10158509041017550.
8. Donald J. Trump (@realDonaldTrump), "'Breaking News: In Pennsylvania there were 205,000 more votes than there were voters,'" Twitter, December 28, 2020. https://twitter.com/realDonaldTrump/status/1343663159085834248.
9. Quoted in Josh Shapiro, "Not Breaking News: Trump Is Tweeting Nonsensical Lies Again," Twitter, December 28, 2020. https://twitter.com.
10. Quoted in Louise Hall, "Twitter Immediately Flags Trump's First Six Tweets as Misleading on Day After Biden's Win," *The Independent*, November 8, 2020. www.independent.co.uk.
11. *New York Times Co. v. Sullivan*, 376 U.S. 254 (1964).

12. *Cantwell v. Connecticut*, 310 U.S. 296 (1940).
13. Quoted in Justia, "*Packingham v. North Carolina*, 582 U.S. (2017)." https://supreme.justia.com.
14. Quoted in Marcy Gordon, "Twitter, Facebook CEOs Vow Election Action; GOP Touts Curbs," Associated Press, November 17, 2020. https://apnews.com.
15. Quoted in Lauren Feiner, "Mark Zuckerberg and Jack Dorsey Testify Before the Senate Tuesday," CNBC, November 17, 2020. www.cnbc.com.

Chapter Two: Forum for Hate

16. Quoted in Rakib Ehsan and Paul Stott, *Far-Right Terrorist Manifestos: A Critical Analysis*. London: Henry Jackson Society, 2020, p. 12.
17. Lexico, s.v. "hate speech," *Oxford English Dictionary*, 2021. www.lexico.com.
18. British Institute of Human Rights, *Mapping Study on Projects Against Hate Speech Online*. Strasbourg: Council of Europe, 2012, p. 8.
19. Quoted in NYU Tandon School of Engineering, "Hate Speech on Twitter Predicts Frequency of Real-Life Hate Crimes," June 24, 2019. https://engineering.nyu.edu.
20. Koustuv Saha et al., "Prevalence and Psychological Effects of Hateful Speech in Online College Communities," Proceedings of the ACM Web Science Conference, September 18, 2020. www.ncbi.nlm.nih.gov.
21. Tarlach McGonagle, "Hate Speech: 'It's the Victim's Perspective That Matters,'" DW Akademie, May 19, 2016. www.dw.com.
22. Wiktor Soral et al., "Exposure to Hate Speech Increases Prejudice Through Desensitization," *Aggressive Behavior*, March 2018. https://pubmed.ncbi.nlm.nih.gov.
23. Joshua Uyheng and Kathleen M. Carley, "Bots and Online Hate During the COVID-19 Pandemic: Case Studies in the United States and the Philippines," *Journal of Computational Social Science*, October 20, 2020. www.ncbi.nlm.nih.gov.
24. *Twitter Blog*, "Updating Our Rules Against Hateful Conduct," December 2, 2020. https://blog.twitter.com.
25. Quoted in Anderson and Rainie, "The Future of Truth and Misinformation Online."

Chapter Three: Cyberbullying and Shaming

26. Quoted in BrieAnna J. Frank, "Mesa Family Didn't Know 10-Year-Old Girl Was Being Cyberbullied Until After She Killed Herself," *Arizona Republic* (Phoenix, AZ), August 6, 2020. www.azcentral.com.

27. Quoted in Frank, "Mesa Family Didn't Know 10-Year-Old Girl Was Being Cyberbullied Until After She Killed Herself."

28. Jonathon Van Maren, "Ten Reasons Not to Give Your Kid a Smartphone," *The Bridgehead* (blog), September 18, 2020. https://thebridgehead.ca.

29. Quoted in Katy Steinmetz, "Inside Instagram's War on Bullying," *Time*, July 8, 2019. https://time.com.

30. Quoted in Sharon Grigsby, "Dallas-Area Teen Who Survived Six Suicide Attempts Has a Message for You and Your Kids," *Dallas News*, September 18, 2020. www.dallasnews.com.

31. Quoted in Steinmetz, "Inside Instagram's War on Bullying."

32. Van Maren, "Ten Reasons Not to Give Your Kid a Smartphone."

33. Quoted in Taylor Lorenz, "Teens Are Being Bullied 'Constantly' on Instagram," *The Atlantic*, October 10, 2016. www.theatlantic.com.

34. Quoted in Sonya Collins, "Teen Suicide: 'The Time for Secrecy Is Over,'" WebMD, July 25, 2017. www.webmd.com.

35. Quoted in Lorenz, "Teens Are Being Bullied 'Constantly' on Instagram."

36. Quoted in Steinmetz, "Inside Instagram's War on Bullying."

37. Quoted in Lorenz, "Teens Are Being Bullied 'Constantly' on Instagram."

38. Quoted in Olga Khazan, "The Millennial Mental-Health Crisis," *The Atlantic*, June 11, 2020. www.theatlantic.com.

39. Quoted in James Vincent, "YouTube Brings Back More Human Moderators After AI Systems Over-censor," The Verge, September 21, 2020. www.theverge.com.

40. Quoted in Steinmetz, "Inside Instagram's War on Bullying."

41. Quoted in Steinmetz, "Inside Instagram's War on Bullying."

Chapter Four: Designed to Addict

42. Tracey Folly, "Why I Deleted My Social Media Accounts," Medium, February 20, 2020. https://medium.com.

43. Folly, "Why I Deleted My Social Media Accounts."

44. Folly, "Why I Deleted My Social Media Accounts."

45. Folly, "Why I Deleted My Social Media Accounts."

46. Quoted in H. Tankovska, "U.S. Internet Users Addicted to Social Media 2019, by Age Group," Statista, January 28, 2021. www.statista.com.

47. Quoted in Gigen Mammoser, "The FOMO Is Real: How Social Media Increases Depression and Loneliness," Healthline, December 9, 2018. www.healthline.com.

48. Dar Meshi et al., "Excessive Social Media Users Demonstrate Impaired Decision Making in the Iowa Gambling Task," *Journal of Behavioral Addictions*, March 1, 2019. www.ncbi.nlm.nih.gov.

49. Quoted in Caroline Brooks, "Excessive Social Media Use Is Comparable to Drug Addiction," MSU Today, January 10, 2019. https://msutoday.msu.edu.

50. Dar Meshi, interview with the author, September 9, 2019.

51. Quoted in Digital Information World, "Reality Behind the Claims of Social Media Addiction," July 11, 2018. www.digitalinformationworld.com.

52. Kareem Darwish, *Social Media Addiction*, YouTube, January 28, 2021. https://youtu.be/CoQtTgIsBn0.

53. Quoted in Paul Lewis, "'Our Minds Can Be Hijacked': The Tech Insiders Who Fear a Smartphone Dystopia," *The Guardian* (Manchester, UK), December 12, 2017. www.theguardian.com.

54. Quoted in Digital Information World, "Reality Behind the Claims of Social Media Addiction."

55. Quoted in Matta Busby, "Social Media Copies Gambling Methods 'to Create Psychological Cravings,'" *The Guardian* (Manchester, UK), May 8, 2018. www.theguardian.com.

56. Quoted in Avery Hartmans, "Jack Dorsey Says Social Media Platforms like Twitter and Facebook Can Be Addictive—Mark Zuckerberg Says the Research Is 'Inconclusive,'" Insider, November 17, 2020. www.businessinsider.com.

57. Quoted in Hartmans, "Jack Dorsey Says Social Media Platforms like Twitter and Facebook Can Be Addictive—Mark Zuckerberg Says the Research Is 'Inconclusive.'"

58. Quoted in Hartmans, "Jack Dorsey Says Social Media Platforms like Twitter and Facebook Can Be Addictive—Mark Zuckerberg Says the Research Is 'Inconclusive.'"

59. Josh Hawley, "The Social Media Addiction Reduction Technology (SMART) Act," Josh Hawley: U.S. Senator for Missouri, July 30, 2019. www.hawley.senate.gov.

Center for Safe and Responsible Internet Use
www.cyberbully.org

The Center for Safe and Responsible Internet Use helps young people keep themselves safe and respect others on the internet. Its website contains information designed to help people learn about responsible internet behavior.

Common Sense Media
www.commonsensemedia.org

Common Sense Media is an independent nonprofit organization that provides education, ratings, and tools to families to promote safe technology and media for children and teens. Its goal is to help kids thrive in a world of media and technology.

FactCheck.org
www.factcheck.org

FactCheck.org is a nonprofit website with the self-described mission of reducing the level of deception and confusion in US politics. The website features a Viral Spiral section devoted to debunking social media misinformation.

Get Net Wise
www.getnetwise.org

Get Net Wise is a website supported by internet industry corporations and public interest organizations. Its goal is to ensure that internet users have safe and constructive online experiences. The website contains information about digital citizenship, media literacy, and online misinformation.

Internet & American Life Project
http://pewinternet.org

Through its Internet & American Life Project, the Pew Research Center studies how Americans use the internet and how digital technologies are shaping the world today. Its website has the results of numerous studies about social media and the internet.

Snopes
www.snopes.com

Founded in 1994, Snopes is the oldest and largest fact-checking website. Its easily searchable database allows users to see what the Snopes investigators have learned about various social media posts and other online stories. Its fact-check articles often include links to documenting sources so readers can do independent research and make up their own minds.

Stay Safe Online
www.staysafeonline.org

Part of the National Cyber Security Alliance, this website offers educational materials, information for home users on protecting their computers and children, cybersecurity practices, videos, a self-assessment quiz, and additional information.

Books

Nicholas Carr, *The Shallows: What the Internet Is Doing to Our Brains*. New York: Norton, 2020.

Mark Carrier, *From Smartphones to Social Media: How Technology Affects Our Brains and Behavior.* Santa Barbara, CA: Greenwood, 2018.

Kathryn Hulick, *Thinking Critically: Fake News*. San Diego: ReferencePoint, 2020.

Carla Mooney, *Fake News and the Manipulation of Public Opinion*. San Diego: ReferencePoint, 2019.

Cailin O'Connor and James Owen Weatherall, *The Misinformation Age: How False Beliefs Spread*. New Haven, CT: Yale University Press, 2020.

Thomas Rid, *Active Measures: The Secret History of Disinformation and Political Warfare*. New York: Farrar, Straus and Giroux, 2020.

Nancy Jo Sales, *American Girls: Social Media and the Secret Lives of Teenagers*. New York: Vintage, 2017.

Bradley Steffens, *Social Media Addiction*. San Diego: ReferencePoint, 2020.

Bradley Steffens, *Social Media Deception*. San Diego: ReferencePoint, 2020.

Internet Sources

Agneta, "5 Things I Did to Break My Social Media Addiction," *Minty Matter* (blog), May 24, 2020. http://mintymatter.com.

Janna Anderson and Lee Rainie, "Stories from Experts About the Impact of Digital Life," Pew Research Center, July 3, 2018. www.pewinternet.org.

Brooke Auxier, "64% of Americans Say Social Media Have a Mostly Negative Effect on the Way Things Are Going in the U.S. Today," Pew Research Center, October 15, 2020. www.pewinternet.org.

Ezria Copper, "The Dark Side of Social Media," TurboFuture, January 24, 2021. https://turbofuture.com.

Avery Hartmans, "Jack Dorsey Says Social Media Platforms like Twitter and Facebook Can Be Addictive—Mark Zuckerberg Says the Research Is 'Inconclusive,'" Insider, November 17, 2020. www.businessinsider.com.

Institute of Humane Studies, "Social Media, Tribalism, and the Prevalence of Fake News," *Big Think* (blog), June 12, 2019. https://theihs.org.

Daniel Kruger, "Social Media Copies Gambling Methods 'to Create Psychological Cravings,'" Institute for Healthcare Policy & Innovation, May 8, 2018. https://ihpi.umich.edu.

Gigen Mammoser, "The FOMO Is Real: How Social Media Increases Depression and Loneliness," Healthline, December 9, 2018. www.healthline.com.

Farhad Manjoo, "I Spoke to a Scholar of Conspiracy Theories and I'm Scared for Us," *New York Times*, October 21, 2020. www.nytimes.com.

Neil G. Ruiz et al., "Many Black and Asian Americans Say They Have Experienced Discrimination amid the COVID-19 Outbreak," Pew Research Center, July 1, 2020. www.pewinternet.org.

Katy Steinmetz, "Inside Instagram's War on Bullying," *Time*, July 8, 2019. https://time.com.

Teens Against Bullying, "Real Teens Speak Out," February 3, 2021. https://pacerteensagainstbullying.org.

Zara Zareen, "Why Mindless Scrolling Is So Powerfully Addictive," *The Startup* (blog), September 3, 2019. https://medium.com.

Index

Note: Boldface page numbers indicate illustrations.